The Shades Of Love

(A Collection of poems)

KEERTHANA SRIKANTH

AELAY PUBLISH

Published By:
Aelay Publish
5/175, Fathima nagar,
Kuthenkuly,
Tirunelveli -627104
Phone: 9944992571

Design And Executed by
And Motivative Tamizha

ISBN : 978-93-5533-078-9
Page : 179

Hey you, who is reading this

You are born beautiful.

Author's Bio

Miss. Keerthana Srikanth, an ordinary 20 years old writer penning her emotions in words. Who aspires to conquer the world with the words engraved on her soul. She writes hues of emotions and inspires people with her words. Her writing journey begins at Grade 10 and now it becomes her passion. She has won many awards and prizes for her writing talent. Currently she is an ACS aspirant and pursuing bachelor degree. She strongly believes that miracles start from within us.

Acknowledgements

My sincere thanks to the following people without whom this book is incomplete.

God, for making me shine and glow with his blessings.

My **readers**, for constant love.

My elder sister and the first reader of my book **Hema**, thank you so much for standing with me through all thick and thins. For having trust and faith in my talents. Thanks for copy editing my works.

My dearest ones **Rubeeka** and **Balaji Anna** for being my pillar of strength and loving me for who I'm.

My **family** and **friends** for believing and supporting me.

Aelay Publication, for publishing this book and making my dream come true.

Lastly, my **Critics** for helping me to improve myself.

CONTENT

- **QUOTES -**

- **POEM –**

QUOTES -LOVE

Want to taste the essence of love?

Welcome to Paradise.

#1

Even the crimson sky felt jealous on the shades of love
bites that blossomed on your warm neck.

#2

Your arms are strong enough to hold the beautiful
broken pieces of mine. You complete me.

#3

Love you more than the moon loves the night and the
sun loves the morning.

#4

"Wake up at 6am with me, when it's still dark and breezy out. Let's secretly romance with nature when the world is still asleep. Let's drive nowhere and buy our favourite flavoured coffee's to make this romance a bit warm. Let's try to guess the flavours from each other lips."

#5
What's love?!
In me, it's just you.

#6
This journey is perfect! I say it's beyond perfect as long
as your fingers intertwined with mine.

#7
I will love you till the sea refuses to kiss the sand.

#8
Current mood?!
All I need is you next to me.

#9
Let's live in love till the deepest part of the earth. Let's
together live the best years of our lives.

#10
What's cute?!
The way he convince me by pulling his ears with a sheepish grin on his face after committing a mistake.

#11
My eyes filtering out everything, other than you.

#12
I will love you till I settle among those twinkling canopy of stars.

#13
"Why are you stalking me? What should I do?" She asked.
"Just fall for me like the way
I fell head over heels for you" he winked at her.
"You are driving me crazy" she blushed.

#14

Even if the blue skies parts away, the muddy land drought, the sweet lies that melts, my love for you is beyond the entity.

#15

I love to be with him,
Even after lights go dim.
I love his fragrance smell,
That drives me crazy as hell.
He never let down my pride,
And that's why I want to be his bride.

#16

"How to burn calories? Healthy diet or exercises?
What will you prefer?" He asked reading the headline
of a fitness article.
"I prefer you" she replied with a naughty smile.

#17

He reads her favourite story book for her during their bedtime. She leans on his shoulder and holds his arm. He holds the book in one hand and rubs her hair in another hand. She falls asleep on his chest before the story ends but he completes their love story by planting a soft kiss on her forehead.

#18

Nevertheless, my constant search to rest my head on your lap. I'm never going to leave your side even an inch or a stride.

#19

She came one step closer to him and looked straight into his eyes "People use to say that life is too short, so live your life to the fullest!"

She sighed, kneeled down and opened the proposal ring "Will You Be My Fullest?!"

#20

"Till how much will you love me?!", She asked.
"I will love you till the wrinkles on your cheeks
disappear", He whispered in her ears.

#21

There is always that one song which connects two
souls as one. The song which is dedicated by your
loved one for you. Just the starting line of the song,
makes you remember about them and bring a glimpse
on your face.

#22

Why my love for you overflows without the realisation
of mine. What's happening within me? Just a thought
about you makes my heart flutter. Why am I yearning
for your call? Why am I jumping up and down when I
get a text from you? An expectation lingers in my heart
whenever you call my name. If these feelings
continues what will happen to me. Will I fall head over
heels for you?

#23

JUST LIKE THE...

Just like a child who picks up the sea shells in the wavy beach, let me pick you up and hold in my fist safely.

Just like the plants getting drenched in the rain, I get drenched by your love even before I look deep into your eyes.

Just like the ocean wishing to fill itself into a conch, I wish to spend rest of my lives in your arms.

#24

THE NATURE AND YOU

Are you a wind?!
Because you send chills down my spine whenever you
caressed me.

Are you a flower?!
Because I blossom whenever our eyes meet.

Are you a rain?!
Because I can't wait to get drenched by your love.

Are you a water?!
Because I can't survive without you.

#25

"What's more beautiful thing in this world?", She asked.

"Us", he whispered in her ears.

#26

In spite of seeing you thousand times a day, still my heart hunch to see you more.

#27

I will love you till the life line on my palm disappears, my love.

#28

Love you just like a romantic song on a drizzling spring night.

#29

With your moonlight magic you glow up the whole sky.
Let's lay down on the grass and gaze the stars until you
fall asleep on my chest peacefully.

#30

First kiss

Eyes shut,

Breathe merged,

Tongue's explored,

Heartbeat raised,

Lips found their home.

#31

"Honey, I need an ice cream but whether I will get it at 2am?!", she switched on the lights and searched for specs.

"5mins", he replied in sleepy tone. He picked his walking stick and shuts the door.

"Here", he gave her the ice-cream.

"Even I would have come with you. Isn't it breezy outside?!", she saw his frozen wrinkle cheeks.

"A little. Isn't the ice-cream melted?!", he asked.

"Melted. But not the ice-cream, my heart", she looks at him with love in her eyes and plants cream lip mark on his cheeks.

The beautiful feeling that starts from your 20th wedding anniversary is pure and truly magical and it's called as LOVE.

#32

Love is when I found a part of me which always craved
to be loved by you.

#33

"What kind of boyfriend you need?"

I want a one who never hesitates to lick the plate clean
after having Maggi with me just like I do.

I want a one who never hesitates to sing my favourite
song in wrong lyrics with utmost confidence for me.

I want a one who never hesitates to lick the chocolate
wrappers clean after having the chocolates with me.

#34

"What's her deadliest weapon? Eyesight or smile?"

"Our chat screenshots, which she often uses during our random fights", he replied with a pity smile.

#35

"Do you believe in black magic?!", They asked.

"Yes! It exist in her eyes", He replied with a smile.

#36

"Do you believe in destiny?"

She asked.

"Only if you are my destiny!"

He whispered.

#37

"What's beautiful in her?!", they asked.

"Her flaws", he replied proudly.

#38

Let's stay silent till the galaxies in your eyes merges
with the stardust of mine.

#39

Why did the whole world melted and turned red when
you kissed my lips by showering all your coyness?

#40

Love is where I ended and you began.

#41

I'm falling for you each second of every minute.

#42

I don't admire everyone. If you catch me while am admiring you, let me know you that you make my heart flutter.

#43

If you love them, tell them.

If you like them as a friend, tell them.

However you feel please do tell them. Stop confusing them between love and friendship.

#44

"What kind of music do you like?", he asked.

"Rhythm of your heartbeat", she said and hugged him.

#45

What's cute?!

When he wipes his wet hair with my saree pleats .

#46

Crush : (noun)

Whom you reminisce while listening to any romantic songs.

#47

Let's camp out in the open beach yard. Let's romance with nature under the terrestrial night sky. Let's gaze at the forest of stars. Let's feel the shiver when salty breeze touches our body. Let me warm ourselves against each other bare skin.

#48

You are the only one, I always wished for.

#49

If a girl is damn rude but still she cares for you. Trust me, you are special to her.

#50

Why her?!

Because I love the way she mocks me, narrates my lame jokes, uses my slang better than me. She is my mini - me.

#51

The hunch of resting my head on my girl's lap would bring me the ease of healing after a worn out day.

#52

Happiness is when your crush says,

"You are the best thing that has ever happened to me"

#53

"Don't lose her" his sister said.

"I won't. But why?" He asked blindly.

"Because she looks at you the way mom looks at dad. She is the one" she patted his shoulder.

#54

Being her boyfriend doesn't mean you have the right to control and demand her to be around you 24/7. Sometimes, even she needs private space to grow and explore.

#55

Parting away always hurts! Either you are ditched or chosen to end all those love dramas.

"Some people don't realize what they have until it's gone, but that does not always mean they are supposed to get it back."

\- Stephan Labossiere

If you get things back as it was, trust me! There is nothing wrong getting back your Ex as your destiny!

If not, please don't go through those tragedies and nightmare once again.

#56

Let me capture the dazzling red pink sun dawn which emerges on your cheek when my lips touches your forehead with a kiss.

#57

My eyes are constantly searching for you. Even if mine met yours why don't you accept your feelings? Just by your presence, I burn like a furnace. Will you spare me or touch my soul? If not, are you okay to see me walking ablaze with your thoughts?

#58

I want to fall asleep in your arms. I don't mind whether I wake up covered with layers upon layers of clothing or our bare skin against each other. All I need is you next to me.

#59

Perks of having annoying girlfriend

Will you watch my favourite love movies with me?
Even if I annoy you by reciting each and every
dialogue?

#60

Your glimpse, a tranquilizer shot on a worn out
traveller.

#61

His face was too close to her that he can even smell
her sweet fragrances. He tugs her hair behind her ears
and she blossoms like a flower. He caught the glimpse
on her face when she blushed in love. He came closer
and whispered in her ears "I love You"

#62

In the early rays of sweet fragrances of spring, my heart craved for a warm place to catnap. The quest became complete in your chest.

#63

Just like the rain which quenches the thirst of the soil, your deadly eye sight quenches the thirst of my soul.

#64

Hey love, even if you put a stumbling block between us, lock your mind with pointless thoughts. Remember, I'm always there for you.

#65

Due to your magical eyes that dances up and down, my heart yearns to flutter more.

#66

She walks tip toe and sat near him on the bed. She admired the way he was sleeping and smiled. She gently brushes his hair and plants a soft kiss on his forehead. She stood and turned to leave, suddenly he grabbed her hand and pulled her closer to him. She falls and lies facing him on the bed. She rests her head on his arms and looks at him. He pulls her even more close that she felt his warm breath against her face. He opens his eyes and looks at her. He tugs her hair behind her ears and whispers "I've been waiting for you to come and wake me up, my sunshine". She blushed and hugs him.

#67

I don't mind of being awake the whole night just to admire the way you sleep. I lost myself completely to you.

#68

You are the snowflakes who dazzles my day and night.

#69

Just like a magical lightening in the starry sky, you appeared before me.

#70

I will love you till I settle among the forest of stars.

#71

One day, he walks into her life. He cups her face, looks deep into her eyes and confessed his love for her. He plants a soft kiss on her forehead and all her deep scars were healed.

#72

"What's your favourite song?!", she asked while surfing his mobile.

"Your voice", he said and played their call recordings.

#73

Let's crawl to the rooftop and watch the stars shining at us. Let's live in love and forget the world we left on the ground. Let's inhale love.

#74

Even if the languages get over, will you utter your love in silence?

#75

The stars in my eyes fallen in love with the way you look at me.

#76

You are my galaxy.

Full of mystery.

I will unlock those with my magic called "Love"

#77

Our memories became the lyrics of my favourite song.

#78

If my love is a person,

Then it must be you.

#79

I didn't believe in an epic love story until I met you.

#80

For the first time I saw the colours of autumn in her
cheeks when I kissed her soul.

#81

Your love is a flaw in my cosmic poetry.

#82

Are you able to hear?", she asked.

"The wave sound?", he said.

"No, our love song played by the cerulean sea for us",
she holds his hand.

#83

Let's wake up early morning and capture the colours of the sky. Let me go deep inside your hoodie and drench in your warmth. Let's stay silent in rhythm of love.

#84

"Let's go home?", he asked.

"Home is where you are", she said and kissed his cheek.

#85

In a relationship, fighting with them is easy but fighting for them is hard.

#86

In the world full of honey and baby, I fell for his MA.

BONDS

Love to be surrounded by your set of people?

Welcome to Comfort Zone!

#1

AMMA Thank You,
For finding my things each and every time when I left them somewhere carelessly.

For buying me another Tupperware Bottle whenever I lost the old one.

For wiping my tears and pampering me whenever I fall.

For believing and encouraging me in spite of my average board marks.

For filling my tummy full even if there is no food for you to eat.

For preferring me over your dark circles while taking care of me during my medical issues.

I know I can't compensate all the sacrifices you have done and will do for me in the future, with just a THANK YOU. But I promise, you are going to have a beautiful and peaceful days ahead.

#2

Best alarm: Mother

From

" Wake up or you are going to be late"

To

"Go and sleep. It's already late"

#3

What's love? Dates or 2am talks?

" Appa's secret 2am forehead kisses", she replied with
a smile.

#4

Friends? No.

Besties? No.

Then what you both call yourself as?!

Sister!

#5

If you had not done these things, then you both are
not sisters:

Stolen her clothes and wore them on your gatherings.
Together bitched each others ex boyfriends.
Drawn out plan of moving as neighbours after
marriage.
Switched off the bathroom lights when she was inside.
Teamed and stood beside each other when parents
scold any one of you.
Stolen her chocolates which she kept hidden from you.
Stalked her crush profile and gave request.
Attends her phone calls and pretend to be her.
Had crush on her male friends.
During fight, bitched her, grabbed her hair, tore her
clothes.
Used her stuffs as if it is yours.

#6

Do best friends change?

From never ending phone calls,
To end the text before it starts.

From shedding tears together,
To giving tissues.

#7

Best friend is a human dairy who knows every
hairbreadth of your existences better than you.

#8

Indian Mother:

Who argues a lot with the shopkeeper for free curry
leaves but we throw them away while eating. And here
comes the mandatory reply

"Curry leaves helps to grow hair!"

#9

Best friend is a one who adds fuel to the fire. But whenever someone bursts out on you mindlessly, they turns out to be your fire extinguisher.

#10

Brother:

Who always believed in you no matter what or how badly you messed up.

#11

Why always should couples be termed as 'Made for each other', sometimes even best friends are 'Born for each other'

#12

How many of you experienced this?

When mom asked you to switch off the stove after 3 whistles of the pressure cooker or to off the stove before the milk comes out but all you do is either forget the count of whistles or let the milk spill.

#13

A gang of three is always dangerous! They love to gossip about anything or anyone at any time of hour. If one of them hates a person, even the other two hates the same person without any reason. When it comes to staying away from home, they open their wings and enjoy life to the fullest.

#14

Female Bestie:

The only girl who pulls your leg in front of your girlfriend.

#15

Inner me:

I'm mature

Actual me:

Still crying when my favourite movie character dies.

#16

When I'm looking at my mobile and laughing alone.

What other thinks: Is she is in love?

What my mother thinks: Are you still kid to watch cartoons and laugh at?!

#17

Indian Mother's Dialogue:

Me: Ma, Water!!

She: The one who is going to marry you sure committed a sin in his last life! I'm feeling pity for your future husband.

Me: Ma, Hair fall!!

She: I told you several times not to use your mobile 24/7!

#18

Indian Parents:

Either Engineer or Doctor, our ambition depends on what they want to become during their teenage.

#19

Just like the old times. All cousins, a small room, dirty gossips, weirdest jokes, cooking disasters, horror flicks, craziest snaps, 2am pillow fights, warm hugs.

#20

Mandatory dialogue – Indian elder siblings

"Amma and Appa picked you from the dustbin"

#21
Life with cousins:

All are same crack heads. And that's why all stay with each other through thick and thin.

If family trip is planned your first question will be "Why cousins join us?"

They know all your dark secrets and give the best love tips.
Family function is like a festival for you! You neither care about the bride nor the groom. You roam around the marriage halls, take endless selfies, have craziest gossips, be the first one to eat the foods, comment on hot boys and girls, party hard and dance like monkeys.

"Amma, let us stay here for some more time"
Their house is your second home. You never want to leave and end up staying night with them.

Terrace be your favourite hangout and special spot. Endless chats, horror stories, drinks, moonlight food, playing cards and at the end of the day its unconditional love.

Your parents trust them the most, more than you.

Vacation = Cousin's home

Car trip be the best. Surfing the playlist, singing together the wrong lyrics and making the road the buzz place.

Even though you don't chat and call daily. You guys share a beautiful everlasting bond. You understand and stood for them always.

Sleeping together in the hall, hitting on each other with your legs and fighting for the blankets.

You guys make others jealous with your cousin bond.

You guys have your own cousin zoned Whatsapp group.

#22

Different kinds of parents on result day

Evil eyes:

They worry more about what the society or your relatives think about your result more than the marks you scored.

Destiny:

They are carefree about the marks you scored. Whether you get low or less doesn't matter to them. It's you, who matters a lot to them. They choose you over your marks. They are practical parents who believes that marks won't decide your future.

Party Vibe:

They fly high in the sky after knowing you are the topper. They set speaker and invite each and every member of the locality and announce your marks. They feel proud of you. The whole day will be like a marriage celebration!

Race loser:

They are the most annoying ones and you are the most pity one. Even after scoring 99 out of 100, they scold you for losing 1 mark and ask you to study more. You die after hearing the lecture and comparison. Their pride matters a lot to them more than you.

#23

"What's happiness?"

"Meeting your childhood friend with whom you craved
to get in touch with"

Men

Let's together unlock the mysteries about men.

Welcome to Chap Dorm.

#1

More than girls, they complement other men's physical appearance.

"You look handsome, Bro!"

#2

Men do cry. They cry while watching sad love stories, when they got ditched, when they meet failure, when they are not able to protect their family.

#3

Even men love to have collection of things. Especially watches.

#4

They don't like their girl to talk with any other boys. It's not because they are possessive, it's because they know things.

"Men will be men"

#5

Why can't they prefer pink over red? It's just the colours.

#6

They fall for homely girls than hot ones.

"Whoever they are, men don't leave their culture"

#7

Boyfriend Vs Male Bestie

- **Boyfriend:**

The one who comforts you during your hardships and wipes your tears.

Male Bestie:

The one who creates you troubles, laughs at you when you cry and at the end finds a perfect solution for you.

- **Boyfriend:**

The one with whom you wear costly outfits, tons of makeup and high heels even though you are not comfortable wearing those on your dates.

Male Bestie:

The one with whom you can be natural without any make up, can wear those loose pyjamas and soft slippers. You are yourself around him.

MOTIVATION

Feeling drained, don't worry you are at the right place.

Welcome to Positive Dew.

#1

Shut the evil spirits out. Dump the toxic souls in the past bin. Light up the candles of dreams.

#2

Maturity is when you prioritize your goals over 2am talks.

#3

Stop living for others. Block your thoughts on what others think about your decision. It's your life and they are living theirs.

#4

Life is truly magical. Just be bold and courageous. But always remember to prior your own happiness.

#5

When you accept who you are, success knocks the door. Don't care about how you look from others eyes. Just be yourself and remember to be happy.

#6

Don't worry about your past. Just remember, everything happens for a reason.

#7

Hi Pretty Souls!

A gentle reminder,

You are not born to please everyone. Just do what you love.

#8

It's enough, you deserve more. Stop living by impressing people because how much ever you express your love for them it's just like colouring a white crayon on a white paper. Just be your 'Beautiful You' , nothing more or nothing less, Just you!

#9

Sometimes even the frosty moon felt lonely among the countless constellations.

#10

In the era of lust and heart breaks, be EMOTIONLESS to lead a happy life.

#11

From: Buying things by checking the price tag.

To: Buying things to her choice and standards.

She conquered!

#12

Don't judge anyone by their appearance, just remember even salt looks like sugar.

#13

When you go through a hard phase of your life, just remember that everything is going to be perfect one day.

#14

How much ever you paint yourself and let go of your originality for temporary people in this cruel world, you will never find your true happiness. People are still going to criticize you, even if you're perfect. Own who you are and don't let anyone define you. You don't need anyone to make you happy, just be yourself. Happiness is within you! Just find it and live your life to the fullest.

#15

The little things which makes us happy:

"....mentioned you in the comment"

"....tagged you in the post"

"....mentioned you in their story"

"....liked all your posts"

"....celebrity likes your comment"

"....you are added in the close friend story list"

#16

Always enrich the colours of your spirit because even the caterpillar doesn't know it will turn into a colourful butterfly.

#17
It's okay....

It's okay if people don't care about you. People blindfolded with lust. There is nothing more beautiful than self love.

It's okay if people don't want to eat with you. Just order Pizza and eat it all alone. You don't need to fight for the last piece, it's all yours.

It's okay to enjoy your life alone. You don't need to depend on others. There is no-one to give you a key like a doll. You don't need anyone to be with you to be happy.

It's okay to watch the crimson sunset and sunrise alone. You can understand what's the real inner peace is.

It's okay to spend time for yourself and shutting down toxic people. It's your life and you know what to do better than other. Private space is not a crime.

It's okay to get jealous on seeing couples. It's worth waiting for your soul mate instead of hanging out with scumbags.

It's okay to be fat. Jean size is not going to define you. Own who you are. Each one is beautiful in their own way. Just raw, Just you.

#18

What's a big deal in men cleaning the toilet? It doesn't mean he is a husband material. He is just cleaning his own shit.

#19

Dear girls,

Stop begging or crying for his love. Instead of that work hard and shine. In future, let his daughter be your fangirl.

#20

Feeling lonely? Not have anyone to talk? Not yet tasted success? It's okay. Great things take time. Just remember

"Life goes on"

#21

Focus and study hard. One day let your signature become an autograph.

#22

Lost many people while focusing on your goals? Don't worry, you are doing a great job. You are on your 20's and not a school kid to waste your time on gossips.

#23

Don't ruin your present by remembering about your past. Choke it out. Remember, no one is perfect. Everyone does mistakes and that's how life teaches you lessons.

#24

Some people be like..

Enters into your life,

Gives you butterflies,

Leaves one day.

And when you finally move on, again they enter. Guys, it's obviously not destiny. It's just to check whether you are still stupid enough to let them ruin your life again.

#25

You know a secret? I'm a magician. Do like I say, whenever you feel sad or lonely.

"Take a deep breathe, close your eyes and wrap your arms around yourself. Hold on for 10 seconds and release.

Feeling better? Felt the magic?

Yea I know. Am able to see your sparkling smile. You are enough for yourself. Have a great day ahead."

#26

"Are you seeing someone?"

"Yea, there is a person I like and he likes me too"

"Are you going to call him for date?"

"No no no... I don't want to hurt myself again"

#27

"Do you like rain?"

"Yea, it makes me realize that sometimes even nature needs to cry"

#28

Removing DP when you are sad? Be mature. What's the use of removing it? Remove that person who made you to feel sad out of your life.

#29

Three things to check whether you are mature.

"No more you wait for anyone to call or text you"
"You manage and take care of things yourself"
"No more you impress or seek for others attention"
Did you strike off all the above 3 things?
Congratulations! You are mature now. I'm proud of you for who you are now.

#30

Love yourself. Stand for yourself. Appreciate yourself.
That's more than enough. 'YOU' matters the most.

#31

When am young my mother use to say

"Darling, don't get too attached to people. They will
leave you one day"

Now those words hits me hard.

#32

Why do you need others love when your heart is fully
occupied happily with self love?

#33

Stop being available for others all the time. Trust me,
when you need help no one stands for you. It is you
who will stand for yourself. Just remember no one is
permanent in this world.

#34

Have you ever felt like giving up your hope on your dreams?

Close your eyes. Just imagine yourself 5years from now.

A successful person, reaching greater heights, and most importantly you are INDEPENDENT.

The hard work of yours will make it worth one day.

So stop giving up. Go and chase your dreams. All the best!

#35

"Do you miss your old you?"

"Sometimes I think about the girl I use to be. But after realising how hard people play with her feelings and her weak personality. I don't miss her anymore. I love this girl, who I'm right now. Who is strong enough to write her own story"

#36

Girls out there! Stop wasting your tears for the jerks. How much ever you cry, they don't even care about it now. Things take time. Trust me, one day sure they will realize how much they hurt you when they wipe their daughter's tears.

#37

Mistakes are meant to be corrected. Not to be repeated.

#38

Guys if I say I'm busy, yea it means I'm busy with myself and living a life I want. During the time I discover myself, enjoy my me-time and become a person who makes me proud of myself.

#39

Looking for inspiration?

Inspire yourself.

Be the best version of YOU.

#40

Feeling drained? Don't worry, everyone goes through this phase. But it's up to you whether you should move on and create miracles or stay there and spoil your future.

#41

Don't let anyone ever dull your sparkle! Shine bright, let the stars glow with jealousy.

#42

Current mood?

To live with nature and music in a quite solitude. Just me and mini – me.

#43

New year To-Do-List

Do what you love, because nothing is more important than your happiness.

#44

From: Table light

To: Spot light

Shine bright and conquer your dreams.

#45

People out there!

Do what your heart says. Focus on your own dreams. Be financially independent. At last more importantly, love yourself more than anyone does.

#46

When you should not enter into a relationship:

"To heal your past breakup never come into a new relationship because you will just use their feelings. It's all about lust and desires"

"After a breakup, please don't immediately enter into a new relationship because it won't last forever and you both will end up hurting each other. It's all about attraction and just a rebound"

"Don't enter out of loneliness because you act according to your mood swings. You are just using that persons feeling to kill your time. It's all about you and your selfish motive"

#47

Unofficial way of saying NO

"…Will let you know soon"

"…let me concern my parents opinion"

"… Maybe later?"

"… Will call you right back"

"… Mmm, kk"

"… It's a long story"

#48

Questions to be banned Vs How you should reply!

- "When is your daughter's marriage?"
From relatives.
Reply:
"Why? Are you going to give dowry?"

- "What's your board exam mark?"
From neighbour.
Reply:
"A decent one to start my future"
- "Any arrears in college?"
From parents friends.
Reply:
"Yea, just like yours during your college times"

The Shades Of Love

- "Where are you from?"
From strangers.
Reply:
"Mother's womb!"

- "Did you put extra weight?"
From known peeps.
Reply:
"Yea, because I'm EXTRA-ordinary"

- "Do you have crush on someone?"
From crush.
Reply:
"Not someone but the one who asks this question"

#49

Gentle Reminder:

Create your own story!

#50

Single: (noun)

Committed to inner soul

Less pain and expectations

Carefree and fly high attitude

No terms and conditions

#51

Ever Noticed?

Some people have time to put stories but have no time
to text you.

Some people have time to hangout but have no time
to visit you.

Time, doesn't mean hours or minutes. It indicates ones
priority towards you.

#52

When black is the most favourite colour but when it
comes to skin why not?

#53

Don't be afraid of falling. Only when you fall, you will
learn and fly high with your magical wings.

#54

It's okay to be imperfect. It's okay to be flawed. It's okay to be messy sometimes. You are a human, not a robot.

#55

Want to feel better?

Then unplug yourself from the toxic relationship, society perspective, self-criticism and unrealistic expectations.

#56

Quarantine: (Noun)

Mondays won't bother you anymore

#57

No one is happy every time. People do cry, people do hurt and it's okay. But what's not okay is losing yourself. Losing your glow and losing your shine.

#58

I always wish to go to a place of miracles. But now I found that place. It's within me.

#59

Let go of your pain. Let go of the things weighing you down. One day for sure you will bloom.

#60

He is not your everything. Even without him, you can shine and smile.

#61

Do you think the stars belong to the sky? No no....

They belong to themselves.

Just like you belong to yourself.

#62

You are the rainbow of your life. So choose wisely the shades which makes you happy.

#63

Be like a Crescent.

Even though it's not complete, still it glows.

#64

My heart is a home,

Don't search for a key to enter.

It's already fully occupied by myself.

#65

Prefer love, kindness and peace in this chaos world.

#66

Breakup is not pathetic.

Trusting that person again makes you look pathetic.

#67

Your skin is not a paper. Stop cutting it. I know you are in pain. You are wounded. The one who caused you the pain won't come and kiss your scars. So stop hurting yourself for others.

Pain

Everything takes time to heal until then

Welcome to Aching Shore.

#1

You know what's painful?

When you are at a stage where you can neither forget him nor move on. You engage in works and distract yourself. But even that distraction remains you of him.

#2

Stop explaining yourself to the person you love each and every time. If they truly love you, they will trust you no matter what.

#3

I seriously cannot understand whether love, hope, destiny only lies in Fairytales. Then why the hell those words exist in real life?

#4

He said he loves me. But why can't I feel that thing called 'love'?

#5

When I'm with you, I feel secure and happy. It's like you and me as Disney prince and princess living happily ever after for a long long time in the fantasy world. Isn't it magical? I too believed that even ours will be a forever happy ending. But never expected this love story of ours ends with a tragic note.

#6

Even the flowers which blossomed in your love shower lost their fragrances just like how your promises lost their values.

#7

"Why are you like this?! Handling all works and pressure", they asked her.

"People use to say that when you are physically tired, you forget everything. At least by this way I can forget him and his memories", she replied in a weak tone and tears rolled over her cheeks. Her tears witnessed the never ending love for him.

#8

My dear loneliness,

Why do you have this much thirst of craving for his love?! I'm completely getting drenched by our beautiful memories.

#9

Will you at least call by mistake? Our memories keep on playing in my mind, will it return back to me? I don't know what to do with my fluttering heart. Whether to calm or pretend not to notice or to understand your love is all about deceit and lies. I'm the only one who suffers hearts of pain? Even though you are not with me but deep inside my heart secretly prays that you didn't fade away with the clouds. Even if you break my heart into pieces, with all my love I once again will cross the skies to surrender myself to you.

#10

Window seat,

Plugged earphones,

Multiple playlists,

And that one song,

Memories ruined her mascara.

#11

The eyes that wore eyeliner, now wears dark circles.
Love has its own way of destroying souls.

#12

Under the blanket of stars, I lost myself while
searching for your love.

#13

Even the twinkling canopy of stars shed tears when I
miss you.

#14

People say that time heals everything. But I have
passionate feeling that it can't heal the feelings I have
for you.

#15

If you can't stay forever, then why do you appear? Why do you care for me? Why do you make me feel special? Why do you make my heart flutter?

I don't know how you feel, but for me it aches here in my heart. It's so painful that I can't even take a proper breathe. I remember everything. Each and every moment we shared together. It's not easy for me to move on.

I cry my heart out to come back stronger but why do I fail every time. Why can't I stop thinking about you. Your smile always stuck in my head.

Please stop confusing me. I can't handle this anymore.

I'm not a toy, I'm just a person who fell for you completely.

Women

Witch or Princess, you are beautiful in your own way.

Welcome to Lass Land.

#1

He realises that you are much happier without him and doing better than he expected. That thought severely damages his head weight and ego. He tries hard to score with your emotions, which leads to blackmail of suicides or trashing your leading life. Just stay calm and composed! You are a strong woman. Never fall again in his trap. Flush him out.

#2

"Safest place for girls? Boyfriend's chest or dad's arm?"

"Mother's womb" replied new born.

#3

"What's the hardest thing in life? Lovelorn or heart break?", they asked.

"Blood stained periods", she replied with a smile.

#4

Why are females always taught to be delicate, silent and little Princess? Chin up, you are born to be a warrior, idol and queen!

#5

Being her boyfriend doesn't mean you have the right to force her for physical relationship. Even her feelings matters the most. Love is full of magic and mystery, don't spoil it with your lust and desire.

#6

Relationship Tips

While you both are fighting, hug and tell her
"I'm sorry"

While she is crying, lend your shoulder and tell her
"You are strong"

While she is laughing, hold her hand and tell her
"You are beautiful"

While she is sad, pat her shoulder and tell her
"Everything is going to be okay. I'm there with you"

When she achieves, kiss her forehead and tell her
"I'm proud of you and you deserve more"

#7

People use to say that women are complicated. No, we are not! We just expect your time and love. If you mess up things, yea sure we are complicated. Our reaction depends upon your action.

#8

"What's your darkest fear?", They asked.

"Cardamom in my biryani", she replied with a foodie smile.

Men's thinks that all we need is love. But sorry, all we need is eating without getting fat.

#9

Reasons why I prefer to be single:

"I don't want him to control me. I know myself, more than he does"

"I don't want to get his permission to hang out with my male friends. I know my limits and boundaries"

"Private space is not a crime. I need a little space to grow and explore instead of spending my whole 24 hours for him"

"Most importantly, I prefer self love over relationship. I'm just busy loving myself as more and more time passes. Trust me, self love and self care never hurts"

#10

When I suggest a series or movie to someone and if they loves it then I take all the credits myself as if I'm the director of it.

#11

Girls Hair Struggles:

- Which side to part the hair is a toughest decision.

- Girls secret ingredient of cancelling plans: Applied oil

- You have perfect set hair while you are at home but when you step out it turns into a broomstick.

- Good hair day comes once in a blue moon.

- Mood swings be their best friend.
  While having long hair:
  "I wish I had short hair"
  After a hair cut:
  "I miss my long hair"

- Too lazy to take hair bath.
  Too lazy to dry it.
  Too lazy to apply oil again.

- Their mood is based on their hair style. Good hairstyles, happy mood.
- Most comfy hairstyle
  Bun

#12

From: Women Harassment

To: Sexual Terrorism

#13

Girls making friends be like "You too like?!! I already know we both have deep connection! Let's be best friends!!"

#14

She pleaded and whimpered under the monster's feet. She cried her heart out, when her clothes where separated from her cold and bare skin. She screamed for mercy, when her cells broken into pieces. "Help!" her bleeding lips uttered. Dead world echoed, her heart. Then she rose up and stood for herself, sure not as a scattered beautiful broken pieces. Her transformation enhances AVATAR of KAALI, goddess of courage. Brandishing a knife dripping with monster's blood. Roared like a lion in battle. She went wild and ate all the demons she came across, so that not a single evil spirit dare to touch even the shadow of female sex again.

#15

"They love to imagine about their boyfriend who never exist. They draw a picture of him in their mind and get blushed just by the thought"

"Never cry in public. Whatever the situation is, they never get break down in front of strangers"

"Surf endless beauty tips and weight loss exercise in internet but never try anything"

"Be best at stalking their ex profile. Even though they broke up, still want to know his well being"

"Best gossipers! They never fail to leave any hot topic. Starting from their ex to her best friends ex, they talk, make fun and endless laughter"

"Someone who never maintains secret. All India radio! Pinky promise be their promising code"

"Never get satisfaction. Well, I deserve something better. It's not my taste. Even after 100th selfie, I need better picture to post on Instagram"

"Love talking to themselves in mirror. They notice their each and every moves. They check their figure. They talk to their boyfriend on phone by looking at the mirror"

"After watching their favourite movie, they imagine themselves as the female lead"

#16
Actual Days Vs Periods

Me on actual days:
Hiii, what's up!!!
Me on periods:
Get lost!!!

Me on actual days:
What dress to wear?!! Jean?! Shorts?! Denim?! Midi?!
Me on periods:
Why don't I even have a single comfy dress?!!!

#17

Me: Sure, let's go out tomorrow!

Next Morning

Pimples: Even am coming with you!

HIS AND HER

Everyone is not made for each other. If you think you guys are then,

Welcome to Destiny.

#1

His phone, Her fingerprint.
His wallet, Her photo.
His record note, Her handwriting.

#2

His shirt, Her fragrances.
His password, Her name.
His notes, Her scribbling.

#3

His insta posts, Her caption credits.
His number plate, Her birthdate.
His playlist, Her voice.

#4

Her pictures, His secret kisses.
Her birthdate, His phone lock.
Her tears, His pain.

#5

His success, Her prayers.
His exam, Her tension.
His ATM pin, Her birthdate.

#6

His surname, Her pride.
His towel, Her smell.
His ink, Her name.

#7

Her insta posts, His comments.
Her wardrobe, His hoodies.
Her lips, His taste.

#8

Her chest, His head.
Her eyes, His world.
Her poetries, His memories.

OH NO moments!

Life teaches us to expect the unexpected.

Welcome to Awkward Spot

#1

When your crush distributes the answer sheets.

#2

When your relatives asks about your marriage.

#3

When your dad using your mobile and your friend sends a voice message.

#4

When the waiter arrives with the food you ordered but places it in the next table.

#5

When you sneeze loudly while the whole class is in pin drop silence.

#6

When your parents spot you on your date.

=

#7
When your crush calls you BROTHER!

#8
When you accidently like your crush picture which was posted decades ago while stalking their account.

#9
"Ask your parents to meet me tomorrow"
By teacher.

#10
When your best friend is absent for the class without informing you.

#11
When you raise your hand for Hi-fi but they ignore you.

#12
When your teacher announces your mark alone loudly in the class.

#13
When your mobile accidentally slips from your hand.

#14
When you are asleep in class and teacher shouts your name and ask you to continue reading from where your classmate left.

#15
When your girlfriend refuses your weekend date and goes out with her male bestie.

#16
When your crush introduce her crush to you.

#17
When you accidentally open your friends voice message in front of your family.

#18
When you accidentally send a dirty meme to your dad instead of your friend.

#19

When your mobile is about to die and your crush
wants to talk to you.

#20

When your dad screams your name.

Valentine's Week

Is she your Juliet? Is he your Romeo?

Welcome to Euphoria Home.

Day 1
Happy Rose Day

Rose is a symbol of love, just like you being symbol of love of my life.

Day 2

Happy Propose Day

"Do you believe in Valentine's Day?"
She asked.
"Only if you are my Valentine!"
He whispered.

Day 3

Happy Chocolate Day

"There are two things that worth melting for. One is chocolate", he said while both licked the melted chocolate wrapper.

"Another?!", she asked.

"Your Coyness", he said and planted a chocolate kiss mark on her cheek.

Day 4
Happy Teddy Day

"Aww, cute!!!", she screamed with love after unboxing
her gift.
"With whom will you share the other side of your bed.
Me or Teddy?!", he asked with cute jealousy.
"Both!", she sealed his lips.

Day 5
Happy Promise Day

"You kept your promise, my love", she said on their
20th anniversary and he kissed her wrinkled cheeks.
20 years back....
"Let's grow old together. Will our love last forever?",
she asked in her wedding gown.
"I promise you that I will love you till the wrinkles on
your checks disappear", he kissed her like she meant
his destiny.

Day 6

Happy Hug Day

"Baby, it's raining. Let's go out and get drenched", she jumped in excitement.

"Let's get drenched from being inside", he said.

"But how?!", she gave a confusing look.

"Our Fragrances", he said and hugged her tightly as there is no tomorrow.

Day 7

Happy Kiss Day

His eyes met hers, his nose softly rubbed against hers, their breath merged as one, he softly kisses her lips and both merged in ecstasy.

Happy Valentine's Day

Want to fall asleep in your arms. I don't mind whether I wake up covered with layers upon layers of clothing or our bare skin against each other. All I need is you next to me.

Am I The...

You too have weird thinking?

It's okay great mind thinks alike.

Welcome to Telepathy Yard.

#1

Am I the only one who falls asleep with earphones plugged in?

#2

Am I the only one who switches on television at the same time use mobile?

#3

Am I the only one who plugs in earphone and not plays any song but just to avoid annoying people?

#4

Am I the only one who listens to a song for the nth time on loop and ends up hating it?

#5

Am I the only one who draws smiley face or write my name whenever I see dust covered car window?

#6

Am I the only one who twists the cream biscuit and licks the creamy side first?

#7

Am I the only one who still asks permission from my parents to hang out with friends?

#8

Am I the only one who watch series all night and goes to sleep at 5am?

#9

Am I the only one who thinks all random shit before going to sleep?

#10

Am I the only one who wishes to marry my celebrity crush?

School Memories

Want to flip the beautiful pages of school life?

Welcome to Souvenir Book

#1

That **millionaire moment** when you sign your classmates school uniform during the last day of board exam.

That **lucky moment** during your turn on seminar when the teacher picks you to bring chalk piece from staffroom, clean the black board and dust the duster in the corridor.

That **artist moment** when you decorate your classroom blackboard with names and autographs during your last day of schooling.

That **detective moment** when you are curious to know what all the events that your juniors planned for your farewell.

That **landlord moment** when you walk around the school as if you own it during distribution of chocolates on your birthday.

That **author moment** when you fill your classmates slam books with love, happiness and promise to stay in touch.

That **poser moment** when you fight with your class teacher to stand near your best friend during class group photo and say widest cheese.

That **director moment** when you give romantic ideas to your friends to confess their love at the last staircase of your school block and name it as 'Lovers Spot'.

#2

When your best friend gives you alone an extra chocolate on their birthdays and picks you up during the distribution of chocolates around the school campus are always special moments.

#3

Writing down song lyrics in the last page of your school rough note instead of taking lecture notes during class time.

#4

"How useless is your online class?!", they asked.

"Just like the snake showed in the Chandramukhi's film!", replied pity students.

#5

We all have that one friend during school life whose parent is a teacher and we felt pity for them.

#6

School assembly is meant to be a place for someone in the school to faint.

#7

Best friends were separated by height order and the students feel pity for the one who stands first because of uniform checking.

#8

Just like how we skip the Ad's in the YouTube, we skip the "All Indians are my brothers and sisters" in the pledge.

#9

Before
One day before exam:
Opening all the subject books and notes. Scanning through the pages randomly.

Now
One hour before exam:
Opening the whatsapp group and knocking the groupies for notes. Swiping the screenshots and ppt notes.

#10

Roaming through the entire blocks to distribute chocolates on birthdays had its own happiness.

#11

School Life:

The goal is to die with memories not with dreams.

#12

"What's the real happiness? Love or Friendship?"

"When credit and debit side of balance sheet gets tallied on the first attempt" replied a commerce student.

Different kinds of music freaks

I'm an Army! Which one are you?

Welcome to Rhythm Concert.

Nostalgic:

The one who always sticks to 90's songs! They cherish the essence of real love. Their nights and travels are incomplete without "Raja Sir's music". Peace matters a lot to them.

Trendy:

These kinds only listens to top hits songs! They don't care about who is the music director or lyric writer. Popularity matters a lot to them.

Depth:

The one who gets touched with the lyrics. They get inspired and motivated from the words of the song. Sometimes they even cry when they listens it in depth. Inner meanings matters a lot to them.

BTS or OST:

The one who is an army. I Purple You. Whether they understand the song or not, they wave according to their bias. OST's choice is according to their K-DRAMA addict. Saranghae matters a lot to them.

Fan base:

These kinds only listens to songs which is either sung by their favourite singer or artists. Whether the song is flop or dry, they just enjoy in sake of their fan base. Cine field matters a lot to them.

Mood Swings:

The one who listens according to their mood. They don't mind of listening 'Kanave Kanave' right after 'Kadhal Sadugudu'. They keep changing and unstable on what to hear that even their playlist gets irritated by their swing. Vibe matters a lot to them.

Memories:

These kinds only listens that one song which connects two souls as one. The song which is dedicated by their loved one for them. Even though the song sucks, they enjoys it to the best.

Morning Notification

Expectations are never parallel to the reality.

Welcome to Authentic Court.

#1

Expectation:

A message from my crush

Reality:

Today's Google meet link

#2

Expectation:

Your mobile is fully charged

Reality:

Your storage space is running out.

#3

Expectation:

Missed calls from bestie

Reality:

Your data pack is over

90's Kid

I don't belong to 90's era but I wish I was one. It's okay, let me rewind the clock and create those memories and you recreate it.

Welcome to Nostalgia Valley.

#1

Fought? Want to solve the issue?
"Kaaya? Pazhama?

#2

Placing coins under the paper and tracing them with pencil. You have a book collection of it.

#3

Whenever you get a Letter Writing question in exam, your friends name is mandatory.

#4

Listening songs in radio is always bliss.

#5

When you get ready to go to school and it rains. Your first work is switch on the television and eagerly waits for holiday news.

#6

You always feel like artist when you colour the pictures in the Magic Pot.

#7

Even after playing with top in road. You break a pencil hook, insert it in middle of the rubber and rotate it.

#8

You love to carry your books in rectangular shape button bag.

#9

Rubbing eraser in your head to suck the oil and pressing it in the book pictures. The imprints gives us a smile.

#10

P.T period = Nails cutting
If not, bite them.

#11

That happy moment while putting brown sheets and Spiderman or Barbie labels in your new books.

#12

Pinky promise be the code of promising.

#13

Subscribing Young World in The Hindu newspaper.

#14

Playing hide and seek, catch and catch, hand cricket, chop sticks, pen fight, tik tik yaaradhu and raja rani gives you Olympic Games feel.

#15

Semiya ice cream be the best ice cream forever.

#16

More than getting beating from teachers you get more beating from your classmates while playing Nikkal Kundhal.

#17

"Do you know, before building our school this was a graveyard!"

#18

Favourite pet during that time:
Colour Chicks

#19

Rasna be our favourite power booster drink.

#20

Love to write in Hero Pen.

#21

Taking out the rubber in gel pen with help of compass.

#22

Buying milk biscuits just for the freebies.

#23

Collection of cassettes and tape-recorder and once the tape got lose fixed it using pen.

#24

Prank on landline be the best.

#25

Giving model poses and capture it in Yashica Camera.

#26

Collection of tazos, Pokemon and WWE cards and stickers.

#27

Carrying Millon Water bottel around your neck.

#28

Chocolates?
Kismi, Poppins, Mango Bite, Coffee Bite, Melody.

#29

Acting cool by smoking candy cigarette.

#30

You believe that the blue part in the ink eraser can erase ink.

#31

Best school game?
Name, Place, Animal, Thing.

#32

Designing our classmates uniform on last day of
school.

#33

Dividing the social studies classwork by folding paper
into 3 parts - History, Civics, Economic.

#34

Ditching strict teachers together.

#35

Why do you need cricket bat when you have exam
pad?

#36

Last page of note book is treasure. It consists of all
your atrocity.

#37

You still don't know why they kept divider in geometry box.

#38

Playing with Word Art Gallery in computer lab.

#39

You are the best dog if you have bitten the pen cap and broken it.

#40

Sketching the history characters into comical ones.

#41

Folding paper and turning it into four cups.

#42

Sharping pencils on both the side.

#43

Revenge game?
Red Hands
And rest is history.

#44

Happiness?
Getting star, ice cream, V.Good in school note books.

#45

Bored in class, then eat chalk piece.

#46

I feel like an artist after drawing a nature scenery with
trees, river, sun, mountain, crow and a hut.

#47

We all owned a kitchen set

#48

Only legends know the trick to win in tic tac toe.

#49

Helping out Dora the explorer to lead her destination
and finding things on her way.
"Mapp!! Mappp!", "Kullanari thiruda kodadhu!", "Back
Pack! Back Pack!"

#50

Drawing scar on your forehead and feeling yourself as
Harry Potter. Pick a stick and cast a spell "Leviosar"

#51

Bought Shaka Laka Bhoom Bhoom pencil and drew our
favourite things hoping that it comes out in real.

#52

Tried calling the phone number said by the actor or
actress in a film we watched. And believed they will
pick up our call for sure.

#53

Devil's won't possess us if we keep lemon, slipper and
broomstick around the bed during night time.

#54

If you laugh too much or your right eye keeps on
winking then sure something bad is going to happen.

#55

If spider bites you, you will turn into a Spider Man!
Tried all the hand movements of Peter and hope one
day we fly by spider web.

#56

We always wish to get collect all the Mandrakal's from
Jackie Chan.

#57

Eyelashes are meant for making wishes that comes
true by placing it on your palm and blowing it off.

#58

Omni vans are the vans used by kidnappers and you
don't dare to go near it.

#59

Applying fevicol in our hands and play with it.

#60

Keeping peacock feathers and pencil shaving inside the
notebooks became tradition so that it gives birth to
more feathers.

#61

Whenever we get into trouble, you will pray for Shakthimaan and believe that he will surely come and save you.

#62

If you hit your head on others head, horns will appear on your head. To remove the curse you have to hit twice.

#63

If you kiss someone, you will get pregnant.

#64

Want to grow and touch the skies?! Drink complan.

#65

If you bury your broken teeth, only then tooth fairy plants another one in your mouth.

#66

If you keep your broken teeth under your pillow, sure the tooth fairy appears in your dreams.

#67

We all have tried to touch the blue flame of the candle.

#68

Tried standing before the mirror in a dark room and called "Bloody Mary"

#69

Tried to stapler our own fingers.

#70

We all have tried to hold our breathe inside the water for few seconds and consider it as Guinness Record.

#71

Tried to touch our nose with our tongue

Rainy days

People adapt to the technology but nature doesn't.

Welcome to Weather Field.

#1

Before:

Singing "Rain rain go away, come again another day"

Now:

Alexa play melody music

#2

Before:

Impatiently waiting to see the rainbow

Now:

Patiently waiting for rainbow to capture and upload

the picture.

#3

Before:

"Let's make lots of paper boat"

Now:

"Let's make a strong chai"

What if things in our bathroom speaks?

Have you ever imagined what if all the things start talking?

Welcome to Hallucination Chamber.

#1

Mirror:

Stop imaging yourself as Miss World. Why do you keep on staring at me even while you are brushing your teeth?

#2

Shampoo:

Seriously? Is this a garbage bin or head? Why do you have this much lies and dandruff? That's why you should take hair bath frequently.

#3

Tap:

You are taking shower bath only right? Then why you are opening me? Didn't you study "Save Water" in your school?

#4

Soap:

Even though you are clean because of me, after using why do you throw me on the floor? Didn't your mother teach to keep things organised? You are doing all these stuffs and if someone falls and blames me.

#5

Floor:

Wow! Here comes our dance master! Seriously you dance like a fish in the pond but imagine yourself as a dancer on DJ floor.

#6

Wall:

You are here to take bath only right? Then in the name of singing why do you scream high? We are going to go deaf because of your singing.

Getting permission for trip

If someone says love is tough then please own a strict parents then you know how hard life is.

Welcome to Mooch Era.

The Shades Of Love

#1

"Amma! All are going!"
Be your first and foremost convincing dialogue.

#2

When you get an intense that whatever you say they
are not going to leave you
"Amma! It's compulsory!"

#3

Amma's usual dialogue
"Whatever it is ask your dad"
And you know it's dead end.

#4

"Who all are going? When is the return? Which place
are you going? Why are you going?!"
1000's of questions pops out and you should be ready
to answer it in one shot.

#5

The vibe around you be like siting and answering
questions in a top MNC interview.

#6

"Last time went right! "
In reality it would be decade ago.

Struggles of spectacles people:

Life is not a piece of cake.

Welcome to Hectic Vibe

#1

You must be extra careful. You can't predict, even
your small move makes the specs fly away.

#2

Most of the time it rests on your nose.

#3

You have a very hard time
while watching a 3D film.

#4

First thought about you in people mind is "Are you a
nerd?"
A group of people is always there to tease you
"Nallu Kannu / Soda Buddi"

#5

Even though you are not famous, your specs be
famous in your gang. All keep on trying it.

What if your mirror speaks?

Mirror is your best friend? Okay, let's hear few words about you.

Welcome to Grievance Cell.

#1

Welcome you! I know you will come here whenever you have depression. No one lends their ear to your feeling right? Okay, scream as much as possible. It's all my fate to bear it.

#2

Oh my god! You scared me. Enough of staring your shitty face. Go and brush your teeth.

#3

Enough girl! I said enough! Is it your face or a wall? Why are you applying these many layers of face power called cement? Are you going to build a building?

#4

What now? Taking mirror selfie? Why are giving such a weird pose? If the picture doesn't comes well, scolding and blaming me? What logic? It's your face. I'm just reflecting you.

#5

What? Admiring yourself? Seriously I don't know how come you are this jobless.

#6

Hey look here, do you alone dress up and look tidy. What about me? Why don't you at least clean me once in a month?

#7

Okay, go now. You already practiced this for nth time. I'm tired of seeing it. Go and perform well.

#8

Do you think I'm your best friend that when you laugh I laugh and when you cry I cry? A big nooooo! It's manufacturing defect.

#9

Girl, please go and cry somewhere else. Why are keep on looking at me and thinking yourself as cute when you are crying? You know what I can't bear your touch up. Checking ever second whether your mascara is smudged.

#10

Even though you act like insane, I love you for who you are. You never give up your originality. Dress up and slay!

Please don't utter!

People, please don't leave me in this kind of situations.

Welcome to Numb Street.

The Shades Of Love

#1
"Ma'am, you gave us homework yesterday"
-Topper classmate.

#2
"Don't you know that you need change to get ticket?"
-Bus Conductor.

#3
"I love you but as a friend"
-Crush

#4
"You are enjoying your life"
-People

#5
"Now I'm going to announce your exam marks"
-Teacher

#6
"You have gained weight"
- Neighbours

#7
"What's your plan after completing degree"
- Relative

Types of Female Friends after you tell them about your breakup:

Girls can perfectly act as both Badass and Fairy.

Welcome to Disaster Jungle.

Rowdy Girl:

The one who fights for you no matter how tough your ex is. Your happiness matters a lot to her.

Drunken Bitch:

Who celebrates your breakup by tossing the drink for your 'Singlehood' more than you do. Your doze matters a lot to her.

Care Fairy:

The one who run behind you with tissues and handkerchiefs. Who offers you their shoulder to shed tears. Your smile matters a lot to her.

Stalker Queen:

The one who stalk all handsome boys in social media and try to hook you up with another guy. Your naughtiness matters a lot to her.

Annoying One:

The one who "I told you before itself, not to love that guy! It's your mistake, so you suffer alone!". Your innocence matters a lot to her.

Witch:

The one who curse your ex to his death. "Sure, he will die as a Virgin!". Your peace matters a lot to her.

Carefree dude:

The one who neither cares about your patch up nor break up. Who prefer self love more than romantic dramas. Your self respect matters a lot to her.

Poems

Turned words into magical spells.

Welcome to Cosmic Poetry.

#1
The World Owes Me A First Love

On the drizzling evening dew I waited to cross the
street,
He emerged out from the breeze and made my heart
fleet.
A magical trance being under his umbrella kissed by
the dewdrops,
For the first time ever I heard the rhythm of the
raindrops.

He taught me how beautiful walking in the breeze
would be,
There is something about his eyes which made me coy
to see.
During the rain trace I drenched over his fragrances of
scent,
For the first time ever I realized this is what destiny
meant.

The Shades Of Love

My senses became alive and thought whether cupid
had sent him,
Wished he could embrace me till the traffic signal goes
dim.
Without any intension he lights up love and stole my
heart,
For the first time ever I committed the love crime I
never thought.

Before I utter he disappeared in the thin air and made
me sever,
I still hope our first magical moment together last
forever.
"There is nothing like your warmth and no one like
you,
For the first time ever I wished this first love of mine
comes true".

#2

Will You Be My Destiny?

All those unfinished stories are again yearning to unite,
I'm penning down all our memories in words in spite.
My heart once again craves for your warm breath,
Will I be able to inhale yours till I kiss the death?

I whim to get once more mesmerized by your eyesight,
And wander around holding your hands in the happy twilight.
I'm slowly falling for you and sparkling again,
Will my love blossom or turns into ashes in the drain?

I desire once again being caressed by you like a drizzle,
And your hands that tuned to stoke my hair as a ripple.
In the crimson rays one step closer to you downing my knee,
"You are the one I always wished for! Will You Be My Destiny?"

#3

Sun Baked Covid - 19

Under the twinkling canopy of stars,

31st Dec 2019 left mysterious scars.

The revolution 2020 stepped in,

Covid-19 injected it's sin.

From dumping the toxic souls,

In the past bin.

To burying the pretty souls,

In the burial bin.

I wish to see earth,

Strongly united in essence.

Not in mere slogans chanted,

By political parties presence.

Families reunited with quarantine,
Giggles tossed with glasses of wine.
Running behind sanitizer and hand washes,
Corona burst into ashes.

Let's warmly open our heart and mind,
Pray and heal our beautiful mankind.
Stay home, stay safe,
Let's shut the evil virus out!

#4

Canvas Of Marina

India's Longest Beach along the Bay Of Bengal coast,
Sweet escape spot for dear Chennaiites to boast.
Watching the beautiful crimson Sunrise and Sunset,
Imprint feet near the Shore after a complete wet.

The fragrant Breeze as drizzles kissing on our face,
Fishermen Colonies and Harbour at the end place.
Watching the enthralling view from the Lighthouse,
Going on Merry-Go-Round and Mini Wheel leaves
amuse.

The moody Winds are high and Blue Skies are
bright,
All readymade and handmade Kites are 'Dealt' to
flight.
Bring home Seashell Memento as memories of
happy times,
An adventurous Pony Rides in the sunning climes.

#5

My Hollow Valentine

Called by different names as Puchka, Golgappa,
Pakodi,
Merged by one emotion "Bhaiya! Ek plate PaniPuri!"
Originated in the Magadha region of The India,
Heart of the city is our favourite panipuri area.

The Tikka, Khatta and Meetha hot bite,
Filled with lots of spices that lifts our mood bright.
Hollow crispy balls dipped in flavoured Tamarind
Water,
Eating Sukha Puri completes the process shorter.

Spicy Tangy Water and Sweet Chutney slide,
Stuff Smashed Potatoes and Bondhi inside.
Bhaiya! Extra Poori! Extra Pani! Extra Sev!,
For your pani poori my tongue is slave!

#6

Hues Of Emotions

Tokyo Olympics is just a glance away,
Let's cheer up India with drumroll and pray.
In the green field of aesthetic in the spark of light,
Like a warrior you are born to shine bright.

With everlasting love we always believe in you,
Sending fate and good luck to the athletes in the crew.
Millions of eyes watching your game,
Rise like Phoenix and roar Team India name.

You are ahead of all and playing well,
We witness the fear in the eyes of opponent as well.
We join hands to support you irrespective of religion,
You be the talent and pride of the nation.

You carry Indian Team name in your chest,
We are there for you so do your best.
Show the world what you can blowup,
Spread your wings and lift the Olympic cup.

#7
You Are My Secret Wish List

There are countless things I wish to do with you.
I wish to hide in your closet while we play PeekABoo.
I wish your fragrances drench over me while hugging
you,
And together lay on the grass watching the evening
dew.

I wish to sleep beside and admire you the whole night,
Still my heart yearns to see you even more in spite.
I wish to wake while your warm breath against my
face,
And surrender myself completely to you without any
trace.

I wish to love you till the sea refuses to kiss the sand,
And let's walk near the shore together holding hand.
I wish to kiss you under the twinkling canopy of stars,
And let the ecstasy heal all our deep scars.

I wish to cook breakfast for you while you are still in
bed,
And together watch the crimson sunset on evening
wed.
I wish to look into your eyes and say I Love You,
Like a barren desert that has never seen the autumn
dew.

Book Description:

"A cosmic book which enhances the shades of people's emotions. Life is a mystery and every moment is magical. We crave for more and forget to appreciate the little miracles happening to us. This book is written to make you taste the various essence of YOURSELF. We all are like a moon. Wondering how? Then flip the pages of the book"

Here is the spell:

"We all are like a moon. It goes through different phases like full moon, gibbous and crescent. Just like that even we go through happiness, love and hardship. But remember, moon never loses its shine and glows until new moon. So let's all shine and glow till our end"

The Shades Of Love